Women In Love

Poetry That Spoke When Words Fell Short

Mira

Made with ❤ on the BookLeaf Publishing Platform
www.bookleafpub.in
www.bookleafpub.com

Dedication

"To the love that changed me—you are here in these words, in every verse, in every feeling."

Preface

"Love is a feeling, a journey, a longing that changes us in ways we never expect. This book is a collection of emotions, of moments where love felt like home, and moments where it felt like distance. Each poem is a reflection of my heart—sometimes overflowing with joy, sometimes aching with longing, but always honest. I write not just for myself but for everyone who has ever loved, who has ever been lost in the magic of someone's presence, or found themselves in the silence of their absence. If you have ever felt love in its rawest form, then these words are yours too. May you find a piece of your own story within these pages."

Acknowledgements

"This book wouldn't have been possible without the love that inspired every word. To the one who unknowingly became the muse of these poems—you are the reason these emotions found their way to paper. To my friends and loved ones who encouraged me to write, even when I doubted myself, your belief in me means everything. And to every reader who picks up this book, thank you for letting my words be a part of your journey. May love always find you, in ways that make you feel seen, cherished, and whole."

Found

I would not say I have never seen someone more
charming than him,
but I would say I have never seen someone more
innocent than him.

I would not say he is smarter than me,
but I would say he knows me better than I know myself.

I would not say I can't stop thinking about him,
but I would say I don't want to stop thinking about him.

I would not say I blush when I see him,
but I would say I don't need blush when he is around.

I would not say the world is brighter with him near,
but I would say the stars align when he smiles.

I would not say I have fallen in love,
but I would say
can I please see you in front of me every time I open my

eyes?

I found you like leaves find raindrops
and end up looking even more beautiful.

That Night

How beautiful that night was

Soft music wove through the air,
stars blinked, whispering the secrets of our hearts to one
another,
wanted to be witnesses of our love from the sky.

The world faded, just us in sight,
that glow of silver in your eyes
drew us deeper into the moonlight.

The night was quiet yet so alive.
I spoke my heart,
uncertain, yet full of hope.

Then you turned eyes deep as the sea,
and with a smile, you set me free.

The air seemed heavy with unspoken promises,
we gave to each other.

Love was not born that night
it had always been there,
waiting to be known.

Talking To You

You say I don't speak much about us,
but when you look at my face mid-conversation,
I lose the strength to speak before you.

When you hold my hand,
I lose the strength to walk further with you.
When you look into my eyes,
I lose sight of the world around me.

When you tuck my hair behind my ear,
I feel lost
even in the crowd of millions.

When you see me and smile,
I lose myself, again and again,
in that fleeting moment of life.

You think I don't talk much,
but my love for you steals my words,
making me lose myself in your charm.

People say I'm a good speaker,
but I deny that truth
for when you speak,
I lose myself in you, again and again.

I Am Here—Close but Far

I see you as my moon among the stars,
but would you ever notice me
just a pebble in the river?

I see you as my sun among a million planets,
but would you ever see me
an unwanted shooting star in the sky?

I see you as the light in everyone's eyes,
but would you ever find me
a mere speck of dust in the darkness?

We are so close, yet so far apart.
I search for you in every corner of life,
but would you ever take a step beyond
to search for me?

Can the moon see the pebbles?
Can the sun see a falling star?
Can light ever notice the darkness?

Can you see me?

You for Me

You are that beautiful dream
I never want to wake from.

You are that sweet truth
too precious to be shared with the world.

You are that breathtaking sight
I could lose myself in a thousand times over.

You are that golden morning
that makes even the sun jealous.

You are that rare wonder,
unmatched, untouched, unforgettable.

You are that precious blessing
I wish to carry with me in every lifetime.

You are that cherished thought
that lingers even in the quietest moments.

You are that pure love,
the kind poets write about,
the kind my heart knows it will never let go.

Insecure

They say I'm insecure—afraid of losing him.
I say I'm insecure—afraid of losing a part of me.

They say I'm insecure—worried he'll walk away.
I say I'm insecure—what if he never comes back?

They say I'm insecure—afraid he'll talk to other girls.
I say I'm insecure—what if one day, he stops talking to
me?

They say I'm insecure—always wondering where he is.
I say I'm insecure—hoping he's not facing life's struggles
alone.

They say I'm insecure—expecting too much effort from
him.
I say I'm insecure—what if I miss even the smallest
chance
to show him how much I'm into him?

I am not insecure about him.
I am insecure about the way people say
love only lasts when a man loves more.

Can I love you more?

A Month of You

I know it's only been a month, but lately, I could not
focus on my days,
Because I didn't know how you look when sunrise meets
your morning charm.
Do your eyes hold the soft breeze, the golden glow of
morning?
Does the sunlight kiss your eyes, or does the gentle wind
make your wavy hair fly ?

I didn't know how you would look with your hair
undone,
messy in bad or touched by the sunlight.
Does it wild and free like the ocean
Or is it like a river, calm as it can be?

But today, I saw your face in the golden morning,
And suddenly, I needed to know
Has the sunshine ever fallen for you, too?

Stay for Five More Minutes

I know it's been a while since we've been talking,
but please stay for five more minutes
because right now, I feel like home.

I know you have work to do,
and I don't mean to be a burden,
but I'd feel at peace if you stayed just five more minutes.

I know you're getting late,
and I don't mean to be selfish,
but please stay a little longer
I haven't convinced myself to let you go, even for a
moment.

I know you need to leave,
and I'm not trying to hold you back,
but please, just five more minutes
because here, with you, I feel like home away from
home.

I know going home is important,
and I don't want to seem selfish,
but...

Can you please stay for just five more minutes?

Can We Open Up a Little More?

I don't know what's holding me back,
what keeps me from stepping forward
and speaking the feelings I carry.

There's so much on my mind

Is it the weight of society and its boundaries,
or the quiet hesitation within me?

Is it the noise of the world outside,
or the fears I've built inside myself?

Is it the voices of my friends,
or the insecurities I whisper to myself at night?

Is it the shadow of my past,
or the uncertainty of my future?

Can you hold my hand,

look into my eyes,
and understand me—without a single word?

Can we silence these endless thoughts
that spin through my mind,
chasing answers that only courage can give?

Can we, just for a moment,
forget everything else
and create a little magic?

Is It Too Much?

I'm standing alone in my room,
and a random thought of you drifts in.

Do love and effort always have to be equal?

If I care for you more than you care for yourself,
would that be too much?

If I feel for you more deeply than you feel for me,
would that be too much?

If I buy you more flowers than you ever buy for me,
would that be too much?

If I reach for your hand before you reach for mine,
would that be too much?

Would it be too much if I ask you out before you do?
If I wake up early just to make you breakfast?

If I pamper you like a child,
noticing and tending to even the smallest things?

If I hand you your keys and phone before you leave,
just to make sure you have everything you need?

Would you find it overwhelming?
Would you feel suffocated,
as if I never leave you alone for a second?

Or would you take me for granted,
as the world often warns—that when a woman loves too
much,
a man stops cherishing her?

Can I love you this way, with all my heart,
or should I step back,
give you space,
and let love grow at its own pace?

Is this too much for you...
or is this just love?

I'm Not Missing You

I'm not missing you,
but when I woke up today, my eyes searched for you
before they even opened.

I heard your whisper in the air,
pulling me gently from my dreams.

Before I could thank God for another day,
before my lips could speak a single prayer,
your name was already there

Somehow, my hands moved on their own,
fingers tracing the familiar path to send you a good
morning,
as if my heart knew before my mind did.

I'm not missing you,
but every part of me is still reaching for you.

Will It Affect You?

There will always be someone
who makes you feel more special than I do
but will it change the way you see me?

Maybe, one day, I won't understand you,
lost in my own battles,
while someone else makes you smile.
Will it pull you away from me?

Maybe, I won't be in the room,
and I know how easily you light up a crowd,
but in that sea of laughter and familiar faces,
would you still search for me?

They say love fades,
that people become less captivating with time.
But will that happen to you? To us?

Or will you prove them wrong,
prove me wrong,

and show me that love—our love—
was always meant to stay?

22

I Have Seen Myself in You

I have seen myself blushing,
whenever you joke and make those cute faces.

I have seen myself happiest,
when you hold my hand
like the sea cradles the river within.

I have seen myself lost,
when I don't get to see you,
like a fish stranded without water.

I have seen myself complaining,
when you're not around,
as if the world suddenly feels too quiet.

I have seen myself restless,
tossing and turning in your absence,
as if sleep refuses to find me without you.

I have seen myself weaker,

when your smile is nowhere near
because somehow, it's the light that lifts me.

I have seen myself in ways I never did before,
all because I have seen myself in you.

Have We Met Before?

We met just recently, yet why does it feel
Like I've known you for centuries, like world is in our
favor?

I saw your eyes not long ago, yet they flashback in my
mind,
An unsolved mystery, a whisper my heart crave to
understand.

I heard your voice for the first time, yet it echoes in my
ears,
Familiar, as if it has whispered to me through lifetimes.

I watched you blink just once, yet in that moment,
it felt like the whole world paused for a moment.

Have we met before ?
Maybe in another life, or in another world?
Maybe in some distant galaxy, infinity away?
Were we flowers blooming side by side,

Or waves together in an endless ocean?

Tell me
Is this our fate, a forgotten past, or just the magic ?
Because I swear, I've felt your soul somewhere before.

Can You Still Hear Me?

I know this time is hard,
And maybe even more harder because of me.
I never meant to hurt you, but i cant help it

still here I am, calling you from far
Please, don't go too far.

With every breath I take,
My heart counts on you to keep it steady.
Without you, my mind feels uncertain,
Like a wanderer lost in a desert with no end.

My heart feels paused,
Like an empty room.
My ears search for your voice in the silence,
My eyes blur the world without you in it.

Can I come to you?
Can I speak to you, even for a moment?
Can I steal just a glimpse of you?

I swear, I won't interrupt.

I just need to know you're still there.

It's Only Been a Day

It's only been a day since things fell apart,
still here I am, feeling lost without you.
It's not that I need to see you every moment,
But I can't face the silence when you're angry.

Do you know someone is restless in this phase?
Do you know someone is waiting, hoping,
Wishing for just one word from you?
Do you know how someone's world feels so empty
without you?

I know it's just a day, but trust me,
It seems like centuries between us.
My mind spins stories that never happened,
Hurting itself in the absence of your voice.

Do you know someone is mad for you?
Do you know your smile is someone's safe place?
Do you know your laughter is the light someone
searches for?

Yes, that someone is me without you.

I Don't Know, But I Know

I don't know what the purest form of love is,
But I know I can't think of my life without you.

I don't know the seven stages of love,
But I know I'll stand by you, no matter what.

I don't know how love is meant to feel,
But I know the feeling of sleepless nights when we fight,
and the happiness of my heart when i see you.

I don't know how it feels to be loved by someone,
But I know the sacrifices we make when loving someone.

I don't know if love is written in our fate or not,
But I know every path I take, it leads me back to you.

I don't know if forever truly exists or not,
But I know, if it does, I want it with you.

Timeless Us

Our conversations are timeless,
like stars and moon.

We are timeless,
Unchanged in a city full of fake faces.

Like the sea
Deep, beautiful, and forever loved for its waves and
voice,
We move, we crash, we rise again.

in this journey of us, I've come to realize
We aren't just here to find someone we like,
We are here to find the one
Who helps us discover ourselves first.

And do you know the beauty of us?
We are loved,
We are cared,
We are held

No matter how dark the storm gets,
No matter how heavy the days are.

That's us.

The Beauty in Absence

The beauty of love
Is not just the presence of someone
It's even more deeper in their absence,

you fill the silence around me
no matter where i am
thinking of you makes me feel you with me.

I miss you smile beside me,
And still, I imagine forever
With your laughter dancing in my mind.

I see you for moments,
But your words echo in my ears
Long after you've gone.

We build memories in seconds,
But I replay them
On repeat Like i play my favorite song.

Even the darkest worries fade,
When your name whispers its way into my ear.

There's magic in this stage of love
I see you everywhere,
And when I close my eyes,
You're already here with me.

If You're the One

I've seen the world
its storms,
its seasons,
its shifting faces.

I've stood in the eye of chaos,
watching everything I knew
collapse like sandcastles in the tide.

But nothing hit me like this
like feeling the soul of someone
before touching their skin.

For the first time,
I felt alive
like the universe had been
quietly writing your name
into every chapter of my story.

The Almighty,

with gentle hands,
keeps pushing me toward you
as if you've been mine
since before time began.

And now that I'm standing in this moment,
I'm not scared anymore.
The doubts are fading,
the noise is quiet,
and your path toward me
is growing stronger
with every beat of the universe.

It feels like the stars
have handed me a signed promise
a cosmic stamp that says:
This love is meant.

If you're the one
I'm not letting you go.
Not this time.
Not in this lifetime.

Because maybe,
just maybe,
I've been waiting for you
my whole life.

The Only Story I Want

There's no story I love to hear
unless it's ours.

I love the sea waves...
Do you know why?
Because they remind me of your wavy hair,
dancing freely with grace and rhythm.

I love watching the sun dip into the horizon...
Do you know why?
Because it reminds me of your eyes
glowing and full of light

I love the orange sky at sunset...
Do you know why?
Because it mirrors the beauty you carry,
effortless, soft, and impossible to ignore.

I love the beach winds brushing past me...
Do you know why?

Because they feel like your breath
gentle, fresh, calming like home.

And if you are the sea
I am walking toward you,
blindfolded, barefoot,
with no fear in my heart.

Because I know...
this sea is my home.
You are my home.

What If I Tell You...

What if I tell you...
I've been waiting for you my entire life?

That I've searched for you in every stranger's face,
like I'd lost a piece of myself I couldn't explain.

What if I tell you...
there were nights I sat in a dark room,
tears falling,
wondering why I couldn't find you
why I felt so incomplete?

I wrote your name
without even knowing it was you.
I painted your presence
in every poem, every prayer, every quiet moment.

And now that I've found you...
Can I come to you?
Can I sit beside you and finally breathe?

Can I tell you how long I've waited
if it doesn't overwhelm you?

Can I share the darkest storms I faced,
the ones I silently fought
without your hand in mine?

Take my hand now.
Hold it tight.
And just say
you're here,
you see me,
and you're not going to leave.

Because now that I've found you...
I don't want to lose you.

Colors of You

I've heard that love comes in many colors
but I only knew the emotional ones,
the silent shades of longing and waiting.

But then you came along,
and suddenly, I started seeing it
all the best colors love could ever bring.

You turned my heart into cherry blossom
soft, bright, alive
blooming every time you're near.

You make my cheeks blush pink
with every word, every smile,
as if love is painting me softly.

No, I may not know every color love holds,
but I've felt the best ones
because they all showed up in you.

And now...
can I save your contact in my phone as **"Mine"?**
And let the colors of us forever intertwine?

www.ingramcontent.com/pod-product-compliance
Lightning Source LLC
LaVergne TN
LVHW010021200726
843495LV00015B/1862